ALEHOUSE SONNETS

Alehouse Sonnets

Norman Dubie

University of Pittsburgh Press

Acknowledgment is made to the following publications in which some of these poems first appeared: *Confluence*; *Goddard Journal*; *The Horsehair Sofa*, a *Goddard Journal* publication; and *The Iowa State Liquor Store*.

Grateful acknowledgment is made to George Starbuck, Frederick Will, and Roger Weingarten for their encouragement in the finishing of this manuscript.

For My Wife

CONTENTS

I

II

III

I

There are some who fancy the Corn Bill the root of all evil, and others who trace the miseries of life to the practice of muffling up children in night clothes when they sleep or travel.

William Hazlitt

The House of Call

Doctor Darling will care for me and bring strictures
to my throat to curb the drinking, and I will
be a milksop in chase of some clotted cream.
(The ale in the bowl of my pipe has put the fire out.)
We live for an infusion of malt with hops,
the houses of call; and pray for a lucrative post
in the Court of Bankruptcy.
Here, beneath the table on the boards,

there is a little parade of Tory dukes
and kings. And I'll knot together the shoestrings
of each and every gentleman, my dear companions.
Once in an orchard at Burford Bridge I thought
I should like to be put through a cider press.
And this drink works on us like a stomach pump,
getting our swallowed emotions up, what poisons us.

Hazlitt at the Bench, Gravesend

1

Two gentlemen drop us with their gig, a near miss;
William, brush down your trousers and if you intend
to continue with the drinking let's leave the streets.
Mrs. Hazlitt has put up in Exeter, and you at
the Arms. You meant to take the child from school
at the half-quarter. And forgot. Your head
is an alehouse decorated with pine boughs: an inch
of sawdust, stewed

platters of carrots and onions, and the cedar closets.
No, divorce is not an easy thing. Write to the child
this evening. And, for God's sake, let him know
the worst. Those two gentlemen
in their gig, they're wailing at us, William.
Let's step up into that Flemish docke, the oak cage:
give testimony and kill our tapeworm on the spot.

4

2 *The Blackwood Boys as Pederasts Courageous*

The winter breath of hogs calls us
to the border. March Hare,
oh sure, we tap the immature.
Our faces ugly from the crease
of pillowcase or slip, sleep is a slow
burn across our cheeks. On a snowbank
Aristophanes conducts his frogs,
their fatty legs require just a little

spice and flour. The stockades
are filled with choirs. (So begins
this running gun battle between
the shins of boy sopranos.)
Security at the gate is strict; beware,
the hot wire, its vaseline kyrie, as
carefully the 9-inch keeps its interval of fire.

Harvest

Hazlitt, I live in a Quonset hut, an old army
barrack made of pressed corn husks,
and my wife and I eat our daughter's fingernails
for nourishment and to be certain she doesn't
scratch her eyes out. I say this lest
you forget that this was our last humid succotash.
Haydon should have put Wordsworth's head
in *The Last Supper*, or anywhere that he'd be fed.

(He would make havoc of half of a Cheshire cheese.
He toils not, neither does he spin,
and there is a struggle of the will with circumstances.
Do we smell the cod and mackerel: the fish markets of Boston
interest us, as they always did.) Hazlitt, you're a critic;
you go out of town to forget the town.
I go out of life to feed a wife and daughter.

These Few Evaporations of Despair

For 'Ces

Your wife Sarah had ham for dinner, is a passenger
on the Glasgow steamer and is so restless; as if
she should go mad; and could not swallow, she was
so choked. She misses the meadows of Winterslow.
Yesterday, the lynchpin fell out of the forewheel
of her carriage, two horses collapsed. Hazlitt, let's not
be so cruel to these women.
(The wind broke all of the whalebone spokes

on her parasol, and it was sad.) Let's have
our breakdowns, our holidays without applying brakes.
Let's go to bed with them
without it being just another little celebration
of our untimely deaths.
Let's live with them, and make these few evaporations
work for us like huge turbine engines.

7

Organn Meats

1

Please pass the tongue, the liver and your intestines, my Confederate,
and we'll enjoy these organ meats together.
Isn't war a lovely salt lick, and don't you envy them
their pastures, their last watering places.
Isn't it peculiar how the first dispatch from Austerlitz
will give you thoughts you've never had before, or
ever intend to have again.
Here, you can wipe your plate clean with this pigeon wing.

Let's step out into the weather without our caps, or
wearing ten-gallon milk cans over our heads. Isn't it surprising
how soda biscuits taste like cheese, and we are all
eating the hearts of animals.
Paris under siege served up
whiskered river rats as fat as puppies. And, Mademoiselles, please
save the tails that our Bonaparte might pick his teeth with them.

2 *The Dressing Stations*

William, the wild round plums are falling
and the last lovely glider is coming in
along the coast; the girls in the bathhouses
are bending over to soap their white ankles.
And you had no idea that there
had been seventeen new wars since Waterloo.
First, you ask of dear Clarissa.
(She'll still resist undress like an arm that

is fractured and swollen. You must rip open
the sleeve of her blouse. Your embrace
will be like a dressing of gauze and plaster
of paris.) And, yes, we have new weapons:
tanks, flame-throwers, bomber squadrons,
choking gas with the odour of horseradish, the H-bomb
and our Pope's most recent encyclical on contraception.

The Budget of Nothings

No young man believes he will ever die. It was
a saying of my brother's. And still this vision
of a sudden death persists. Your nearest friends
have quit with you, and all your wives
are waiting at the Scottish border. And you,
with your last breath, reply: "Well, I've had
a happy life." You found order in a liquid stew
of pearl barley and vegetables. And I

may even do worse than that. My wife's
herbs on the windowsill are spoiling; the earth
is black with this, our sixteenth day of rain.
The water pump is calling to her heavy sister
across the field. Soon the barberries will be hung
all winter in the Salem snow. And, Hazlitt, you're depressing:
I'm riding a mule away from you.

The Last Pink Wilderness

Yesterday, at the Iowa Security Medical Facility
three men escaped. One night a week I drive
by this place on my way to teach. And what a place
it is, William; with a thousand tinted lamps, one
great boulevard and a double chain-link fence.
You've heard what happens on farms in our midlands:
whole families are murdered in their kitchens. Even
women and children, as in the days of the Indians.

The men who commit these crimes are in turn put
in maximum lockup as in the cellars of Guy's Hospital.
William, I know that you're English, a foreigner,
but don't you agree with the local sheriff
that for it to be MAXIMUM; to console the mourners,
they should build a wall around it
and put riflemen on the four corners.

Late February at Winterslow

1

My wife comes spilling from the pond
fresh buckets of water for our bath.
The incident repeats itself like waves.
And the thaw drops snow like heavy sacks
of flour from the branches . . .
everything collapses within the woods.
I float with the wreckage to please
her during her confinement with dark loaves

of bread, venison and pails of milk,
skimmed until the milk is nearly blue.
Our nights open, explosive
like the great doors of a carriage barn
spilling dark, angry horses, their nostrils
hot and moist. Her coach races north,
forever towards its point of departure.

2

The white birch are stooped with ice, idiot
children who rest
their obese, rotating heads on low tables.
Fresh manure is being swept from the barns
the tines steaming as things will in winter.
William, let's escape into narrow margins of weather.
The snow drifts with its soft boneless shoulders.
We hide under skirts of immaculate cold,

and swear not to give in to that slow chloroform
leak of spring. Count one, two, three . . .
March straddles himself with his flannel shorts
around his knees, is being examined by winter,
the steel fingers of the bloused surgeon
hoisting like a forklift under his testicles
as he is instructed to cough, and cough again.

Address to the Populous Winter Youths

For Dudley Laufman

Hazlitt, we've stepped into the Shaker kitchens;
God's kingdom becomes a pie, dumplings
or the dainty flummeries. You recognize
the wooden utensils and skeins of yarn or flax.
What this faith taught was a heaven on earth.
With no war, no jails, no poor
and no saloons. Only Sister Abigail's
Blue Flower omelets. And celibates

asleep on feather beds. The knitting sheds
are built against winter. They drink
haying water or switchel. They rub
their animals with witch hazel and have
no children. Each community
has a common grave, once remote elbows
become the one elbow of the faith. Nearness exasperates.

The Oaths of Calumny, His Overkill

I walk with Keats as far as Covent Garden; he's off
to play at rackets: the boy nursed his mother, and now
the brother, he'll play tennis with a silk and catgut
snowshoe, the walled enclosure. We should murder
the boys at Blackwood. Lockhart marries the daughter
of Sir Walter Scott and he's forgot that I want his testicles
to lend to John on the tennis court. Coleridge, too,
they all hurt us, Keats; we want their meat for

this last Sunday's tournament. My wife spins
all her own sarks and short-jackets or bedgowns;
and now she would divorce me. She rubs
her ankles and her knees with the cheapest whiskey. Arthritic
Sarah rides in a cavalcade of carts, and resents me
being locked up with three ladies in a lodging house.
She accuses me of adultery and excessive drinking.

Sunbathing, 1778

Those bubbles in your rum are filled with eggnog, William;
during the holidays it's good to think of Puerto Rico,
or of the seven tortoises you exhibited in the family
parlor at Weymouth. You arrive
home with a dead black snake
extended on a stick in front of you. You have carried
it through miles of brush as a gift for your sickly mother.
Margaret is still so leathered and brown; even now,

in late December. She is under the mistletoe, and she looks
to you, William. Do you remember her in the altogether,
a bather, just sister and little brother at Hingham pond.
At age nine your father would bring you into
the pulpit with him at the Old Meetinghouse, and
you were struck with his huge King James Bible, spread
like your sister that afternoon on a rock at Hingham pond.

Lecturing the Schoolmaster

William, drink your tea or here, a cheap whiskey;
it's porter for me: this is your brother's second day
in the Charles Street Jail. Please, don't stare, but
look: you can almost see her legs through the skirts
like great oak table legs behind a falling paisley.
There are glosses on the law of the prophets,
and these days remind us of the large Hebrew lettering
in our father's bibles.

You must ignore the young couples in the park.
The rain does abuse these trees, they stand like
schoolgirls opening their blouses in a draughty hospital
cellar, an annual exam. Hazlitt, you're shivering,
take that silly quill out of your ear:
you've been dead of cancer of the stomach for nearly
a hundred and thirty years.

Hate

Hazlitt, you're a pretty man; I've made you
a lieutenant in my press-gang. You think
neither of us hates enough: the world, ourselves.
I'm overwhelmed, William; let's hear those drums.
Listen, old Scattergood, let's return to that
original privacy we had, and ignore old books,
old opinions and old friends. The stomach
turns against them.

You'll say that this throws cold water on
our intercourse. (You're embarrassing.
Watch your mouth. I have another wooden bucket
in reserve.) This all serves us in a way.
You're putting mice into an air pump; you love
to torture animals. Their eyes pop like milkwood
pods along a highway. We're marching every mother's son away.

Our Childhood at Wem

I'll never forget our visit to the Montpellier
Tea-Gardens at Walworth. My father and I
among the box-tree borders and the gravel
walks. All this after five days with nothing
but water, our voyage from America.
My garden at Wem, a kitchen garden,
was surrounded with hot-glowing peonies,
and I would water the rows of peas and beans.

And in April I sat on the sand off Popham beach
and watched my father, after sermon,
as he swam in the Atlantic Ocean: wrestling
with blue seals, even the turtles loved him,
he was a happy man. That afternoon
I got my old-time religion, and I'll keep it
until the seas evaporate into empty basins.

A Self-Portrait

Yes, my teeth are clenched as I present these early lesions,
my full face, and explain that we are all bled white by taxes.
My fluff collar is washed each day by Sarah in wild water.
I am the maniac who will not hear that the war-horse in Job
was merely the work of a mechanic.
I come back to this vision regardless of everything,
save church mice and metaphysics.
My oil paintings dry like the snot or spruce gum of schoolboys,

over the weekend, underneath the desks in country schoolhouses.
Each night I used to watch my father carefully attend
the winding of his watch. When I'm in town, indeed
it is all borne in on me, for who cannot hear
the progress of all those gears and ratchets, the great clocks
in the towers. Back at Winterslow, I eat the stringy beef
and prepare for that last step onto an otiose porch of rest.

II

Hazlitt Compareth His Heart
to the Overcharged Gun

Prologue

The lover waxeth wiser, and will not
die and biddeth happy lovers
rejoice in May,
while he waileth that month
to him most unlucky.
I compare my state to a wheat
in perilous storm tossed
on the sea.

My sorrowful state maketh
me write sorrowful songs.
This is my description of a gun.
And to his love from whom
he had her gloves: I am
that Mom who ate her child
at the siege of Jerusalem.

1

If wakeful air slams shut the window;
if many sighs with little speech ordain:
now joy, now woe, my *chere* distain.
To haste or slack, my pace to less,
or more, the wakeful air slams shut
the door.
If thou ask whom; sure, since
I did refrain Brunet

what set my wealth aroar
(please draw the shade).
It's Phyllis hath the place
that Brunet had.
She maketh me very glad
with white meats galore. Phyllis
is no common whore.

2

Caesar, when that radiator of Egypt
with th' honourable head did him present,
covering his heart's gladness with dissent
and compliant with his tears, as it is writ.
Eke Hannibal, when women him
clean with his behind,
all last night wife Sarah
was not mine.

The mind hideth by colour blueberry
this easy visage, now sad, now merry
whereby if that I laugh at any season
it is only the asthma keeps me
from wife Sarah. Methinks
it is good reason, my nose
a bulb to bring all bastards into season.

3

I find no lease, my landlord is at war.
I burn and freeze like ice
and fly aloft but rise no more.
Good Father, what do you detect in me
am I to be just
another prostatectomy.
That locks nor loseth, holdeth
me in prison.

I am now old. I scrape no wise
nor wherefores.
And yet of death it giveth me occasion
without an eye, without a tongue
to leave my Sarah on the blistered floor
sweeping from room to room
with her only sister, the broom.

Over Winterslow

For Michael

I have a partridge getting ready for my supper,
the fire's blazing and the air is mild for
the season of the year. With my fist I enter past
the ice in this hand basin, and I'm off
to visit the woods over Winterslow.
Our home is built of blocks of stone
that sweat like the poor man who placed them
here, in summer, some hundred years ago.

Your sonnets are as casual as this first snow,
as black squash, a winterkill; what I'd like to hear
from you is whether or not you know that I'm bored
of you. I want to be alone or
with a showy-looking girl. (Have we been married
by accident, through agency, or simply
by the fear of the event.)

Rev. Malthus and the Poor

1

O, Malthus, how could your miserable reptile
performance crawl to such credit. You are picking at
the labouring poor with logical instruments. I should
like to pick your sweet tooth for you with a hundred-
weight timber. You're a fat shit leaving the confectioner's
shop after a couple basins of turtle soup, an ice,
and a dozen large jellies. You are fatted like a pig,
or like two or three geese or fowl.

I'd like to put my boot on you, you parish beetle.
The poor must be kept alive in winter. I should
like to light their places with your blubber.
While the pleasure and carriage horses of this kingdom
eat half of the produce of the soil, the poor
grow lean. Hazlitt, in my district it's a thirst:
a million tongues lapping a million tubs of gasoline.

2 *For Musician Friends Going North to Canada*

The Putnam brothers and their wives
postpone a contra dance; put the bass fiddle
in their converted ambulance
and cross the Vermont state line.
The squirrel guns of Nova Scotia
and the Bay of Fundy tides
conscript these Quakers and their wives.
They'll rent a dance hall for a night,

a church cellar or barn,
and leave the pastor or the farmer
dancing with the mice. They'll light
a fire in a field, and link hands
with their wives;
with the children
they wouldn't have had otherwise.

Hazlitt Down from the Lecture Table

For Jack

William, let's choose a bracelet for your throat,
it could be one of Clarissa's scarfs, a horsehair
rope or piano wire. No matter which you choose
the fit should be close. Don't inflate,
strangulate. That's our motto. The waffle iron loves you.
There will be a few droppers-in like your cousin
and myself. Dear Hazlitt, as a critic
you prefer health to cosmetics, and Leigh Hunt

asks if despite Tragedy and cares
you don't find laughter and fresh air more precious.
Hazlitt, you were very polite, said once "yes"
and twice "no." The lion came, handed
Miss Bentley to the dining room and asked Miss Perry
to take wine. You never roared, William; you just
sat out the stupor in a corner.

The Mussel Gatherers of London

The bubonic buboes visit us this winter
and according to the bills of mortality
they come with the Dutch prisoners
of war. It's 1664. Will someone light the straw.
Pierre Auguste will do a quick sketch
for us beginning with the initial rigor
and the headache which is described
as splitting.

Your tongue is bundled in a thin white fur.
Our first cousin appears stupid and suffers
constipation. Then the buboes occur
and their most common seat is the groin.
Jenny, just before death your buboes
will suppurate and spill down your fair legs.
It will be the last of the bed-wetting, Dear.

31

The Hub and the Oaken Stick

1

William, you've returned from Holland sick
of canals and white houses with girl-servants
outside hosing down the walls. Here,
have a Schlitz. Just sit down
and forget all about those steaming pails
and suds. Let me tell you that I have
faith in America, in her stockades,
and her seawalls of concrete and steel.

You resent the Dutch complexion, their tariffs,
and their cakes of scented soap like those I bought
for you in Cambridge. You've prayed that the dikes
give way, that the Dutch be bathed not with just
a little ocean spray. But that all their causeways be flooded.
(William, a cranberry bog would be a good place
for you. Or, maybe, we'll put you in the stocks.)

2

The crews are racing on the Charles and it was in a clinic
not far from here that they determined she would
have a nervous breakdown. What a diagnosis; actually,
she had infectious hepatitis. It must have been the faggot
she slept with. His dirty points. William, here's a gauze
mask for you. Never mind the ice cream parlors or
prostitutes: she preferred the Common, the green;
the whites of her eyes were gradually becoming

naturalized like the first tomato on the vine.
It left her awfully weak; she couldn't dance,
stayed away from the coffee houses and discothèques.
And when she had to pee, it hurt.
Her skirts were blue knit like those of
a Catholic schoolgirl. The nuns called her Frances.
William Hazlitt, I'd like you to meet my wife, Francesca.

The Unfinished Tuba Song

Hazlitt, we'll spend the night curled
up in a sheep's head like two fat
round worms. Our host is dead
but still warm. Parasites are rarely
served eviction notices.
Coleridge reminds us that soft membranes
make expensive beds
and this night we are sheltered from the rains.

There are flukes in the heart of the tiger
and he'll always regret
having visited our hovel.
William, we have a caller. We won't be interrupted.
The brass knocker at the door,
we must insist, is only
this animal having its death fits and rattles.

Out of the Opera Pits in Our Black Sticky Dresses

Your father's furniture has left the north country,
and come to rest in Bullock Lane. Here's where you're
born. In early April, on the 10th. Just before
we pack it all up again and send it off to Ireland:
the stiff chairs, a deacon's bench, a barrel of Austin ale,
and one pickled tongue in basket. Now, my father is
playing chess with a Polish cook outside Paris,
and here's where I'm born, in Orange County, Vermont.

That was early April also. The 10th. (I've forgiven
him his absence.) The next day my uncle's killed
by Japs, and my mother's milk dries up in seconds.
(I haven't forgiven anyone that yet.)
And it snows for both of us this first day, even though
you have come out of the north country and I
have stayed. Our fathers are away: in Ireland, in France.

Jeopardy

We're into an ugly boat over the river, rowing,
and on both sides of us the horse pastures are white
as bufferin. Down a quarter of a mile
our friends are dynamiting the ice, though carefully
removed to an old grain bin. We're intent on catching
everything from the water, to be nearly rinsed with it.
David seems to have frozen still, his arm
extended with a revolver pointing

at the charge, a dozen orange sticks
of TNT gathered together like frankfurters
in a locker. A single warm shot. And, William,
everything went up including a young muskrat,
surfacing onto the flow:
a froth of tapioca, the fish eggs at his mouth;
he glanced at us and towards the water, returning.

No. 69 du Catalogue

What is this that's first and last and midst
in our thoughts. Is it the start of the promised hangover,
or your recurring nightmare of the Louvre
where you are greeted at the gate not by
a Republican doorkeeper but by a servant
in court-livery. (By morning we'll have
walked a mile and a quarter.) Let's pray
that everything hasn't faded or been erased.

We're under the black bib of chaste, child
Metternich. Damn this ridiculous watering, our teething
politician. Let's sit out the shower in a Cardinal's hat.
First: the Claude's, the flying priest,
and *The Altarpiece of St. Mark* by Tintoet.
And here's the catalogue, a Bourbon publication;
isn't this peachy, William, shouldn't we have an auction.

2

Hazlitt, you're crawling like an Eastern slave. Do you
think you'll make it. We're nearly there
and it wasn't so terrible, very little
was faded or confused. Wait. What's this?
Windows by Robert Delauney.
Look at all these squares, the ferris wheels
and street lamps. William, it's a modern painting.
(So this is what you dreamt of. Are you paling.)

Look, there: a virgin with a bean flower
in Cologne. If you think this is something
you should see *The Quaker Oats*, or what naked squirming
girls will do with a large canvas on the floor. Yes, some
still paint nudes, but have no use for canvas. What's so
unusual, William; tribesmen in the bush were doing this
centuries before Christ.

The King's Advocate / The Bulletin

Sarah's face is pinched and sweats, shifts between the iron
bedsteads, her positive and negative terminals. Her labor
has lasted three days. Her abdomen is plum colored;
the midwife hears a stirring, and predicts that it
will be a girl. We'll call her by my sister's name.
The bag of waters broke an hour ago.
There is a heap of towels in the corner: steaming, soft
and folded like the new born calf in snow.

Sarah has made many oaths this night, and by three o'clock
only a candle flame would exhibit any breathing.
There is an oyster-look about her crotch. And twice
she has kicked all the bedding from her. (She pivots
like a raw and peeled potato in boiling water.)
And I will step out into the cold of the January barns,
into the stalls, to feed the placenta to all the livestock.

Lon. 67 Lat. 42 25 27   Christmas

For my daughter

Your father's on board the Rebecca and Captain Folger
thinks the leakage has diminished. They tacked about,
at six, the wind being S.W.: Boston. Then good
weather and Folger's back for England. He passed
the winter banks of Newfoundland. Your father
confides that he can no longer write: remembers
the squalls off Nantucket, a sea hen, and two gulls.
Yesterday, the poor owl died.

Hazlitt, let us exchange portraits in crayon, and
never tire of playing whist late into the evening.
Let's interfere with each others attempts at drinking
sea water. There's no curfew here. No factory. Let's mail
these letters to our sisters, Margaret and Rebekah.
Father, do you smell horses over the water,
your children are dying of lockjaw.

40

III

They fell out the fancy religions; the three Jews were told off
for fatigue at the latrines. Mr. Jenkins was detailed to march
the R.C.s four kilometres to the next village to mass; because
of Father Larkin being up at the Aid Post, with his Washbourne
Rituale, and the saving Oils.

The official service was held in the field; there they had spreaded
a Union Jack on piled biscuit tins, behind the 8 in. siege, whose
regular discharges made quite inaudible the careful artistry of
the prayers he read. He preached from the Matthew text, of how
He cares for us above the sparrows.

David Jones

Sonnets from the Portsmouth Geese

38

First time he missed me, he but only missed
the toes of this foot wherewith I write;
and ever since it more grew clean and white,
slow to bird-greetings, quick with lice
when the angels meet. An ankle brace
of steel would not be plainer to my sight
than this first miss. The second passed in height
the first, and sought the forehead and half missed,

half falling on the hair.
That was the break of love, love's own fawn
with sanctifying sweetness did release.
For the third upon my fingers was brought down
in perfect purple state; his axe did separate
the hand from the sleeve. And this is why
I write you of my William with my feet.

19

For Matthew and Rachel

The soul's *Rialto* hath its paradise;
I garter curl for curl upon that start and from
my William's forehead to my heart,
receive this fetlock which outweighs a cat,
as purple black, as erst, a Pindar in his eye.
The slim surreal gloomed athwart,
a mouse behind the fly. A counter fart
the blue-fly laid, Belovèd, I surmise

upon thy curl, it is so parted.
Thus with a skillet of smooth hissing fat
I tie your hair back behind your head
and lay the gift where nothing hindereth
and split your forehead with it.
Dearest, we'll lack no natural gas for heat
as you grow cold in death.

31

Thou comest. All is said without a word.
I sit beneath your genitals, as children
'neath the sun, a soul trembles through
their happy fibs. Thou comest and methinks
I need a bib. Behold, I cannot rue
the sin most, but the occasion.
My dear yawning reason.
That you should stand a moment

unministered by my mouth. Ah, keep close
great stomach.
When my fears rise, let your broad ways
serenely interpose. We live for cries.
Brood down with thy divine sufficiencies, bless
these thoughts which tremble like the birds,
now assembled for the pie.

5

I lift my heavy crate like a curtain
as once Electra her horse urine,
and looking in thine eyes I overturn
the bottle at my pregnancy. Behold,
your Sarah,
and what a grief
lay hid in her.
You could not tread on it with thy feet

for that is only legal in the streets.
But if instead thou wait
beside me for the kid to blast
my grey guts out . . .   our quarrels
will not shield thee so,
that none of all the choirs shall knot
the hairs below. Stand back. I am relieved.

Nightmare on the Monroe Miller Farm

So, William, you adore the black Amish hood,
their spotted mares, and superstitions;
their resemblance
to the alarmist hen pheasant of the woods.
You have the honest regrets of any bird
who scares in sunlight: you break from the hedge
and are shot dead in silhouette.
At last, a blonde female bird is falling

on us; and William, your Death Mask
is the subject of what bothers us.
(You explain that once and outside Belfast
you saw squatting on the limb
of a dark oak tree: the very bleached and complete
skeleton of a cat.) You insist that the religious
dress arrogantly in either white or black.

Eating Out the Angel of Death

For Gottesman

Hazlitt, we gather for some more tavern glow
and it's Kit Smart in drag as Mother Midnight,
the four-foot midwife,
with her *Fantastick-Cat-Organ-Show*.
Christopher makes his musick:
tortures the tails of different sized cats,
and spills turpentine over their assholes.
Another round for Kit,

and then he's out onto the road.
He thinks the only way to pray
is to fall down on your knees
laboriously like camels.
Crazy Kit sat in his flannels
and wrote
that a rat had poor cat Jeoffrey by the throat.

A Visit to the Country Doctor

I sleep with the servant girl
under sheets like wraps of bandage,
and, William, I am a man who believes
in death and taxes.
I wear Kleenex boxes on my feet.
The pigsty was poor winter quarters.
I grew sick of those steaming horses,
and I asked only that she wear

an underwaist to lift her breasts
and that she pin her garments.
There is a carriage wheel spinning
backwards within my stomach.
Today, again, Franz heard the landlady's
daughter at her French lesson.
Along with the halt it causes torment.

Sonnet for Lydia Hazlitt, 1872–1876

Hazlitt, the only stain is on the sleeve;
her mother rubs it clean
between the thumbs with kerosene.
The father finds a sane arrangement
for her sisters, leaves them to disorder:
the girls nervous for the powder blast,
the white flash of magnesium,
the photograph.

William, they have her in rose slippers
with a pine bough over her shoulder
for a border. The backbone follows
to the skull like a handle on a dipper.
Last night, the father full of anger
for the cholera cut for her
a pine bough, his grief, a panorama.

The Red-haired Bandits of Mawddwy

1

Takis, on the motheris breast sowkand,
the babe full of benignitie and
this fatigue can be felt by corporals
and trout alike.
The quarter-bloke behind the stars
makes his cushy good night.
A Welch platoon passes us beneath the moon.
We march carefully before the large house.

One night Alcibiades went around town
with a great hammer knocking the cock and balls
from every statue he found. In the morning
the candlestick makers greeted the gods,
all castrated. All congratulated Alcibiades.
This rifle is not light and it makes
for the savage bloke, his million light years of night.

51

2

In this unheated room I'll introduce
to you our last friend, pollination Daniel.
He'll stay until the gas-rattles begin,
until the wooden clappers give
the gas alarm. Then it's back into
the trenches with the talc goggles
and *A'r gath wedi crufu Joni bach.*
There are mudhooks in our socks

and the excellent canvas stretchers are before us.
Woodrow is the patroness of the gunners,
even though he's had that awful stroke
and the crazy bloke is just a sandbag to us.
The wives listen to the broadcasts;
the last letter-bell announces pollination Daniel,
his wooden rattle entertains the children.

Hazlitt on His Sickbed
For G.S.

William, there's a lake bottom in the Catskills
that was used as a graveyard
by Murder Incorporated: there were thugs
brought down by machine guns, their heads
like sieves, their bare feet were set
in blocks of wet cement, and later
they were tossed over the sides
of rowboats. In just that way, we want

to be dropped to the floor of that lake
to be company to those several dozen
lonely figures in faded suits,
and to be kept almost erect
by the currents; swaying
on our pedestals, yet standing meekly
on our ankles, not on our own two feet.

Noli Me Tangere

1

Hazlitt, it's our birthday, the 10th of April
and will we ride the Bath mail, shotgun
in the downpour without umbrellas, the Royal
mail that speeds us to the fight.
The inn at Bristol will give us beefsteaks
and ale as our favorite bare fisted pugilist
eats raw eggs with rum. That's gusto, William,
and we love him.

Listen to him breathe as he runs through the country,
like our fathers in middle sermon; both of them
are dissenting preachers and both boxed in Boston.
We have these seats just outside the ring,
and I'll have another nosebleed and leave.
This day was beautiful, our birthday: to remember
our fathers, and that we were sons.

2

For Goldensohn

We are nude so that our clothes may dry,
reading the *New Eloise* at the inn at Llangollen;
sucking a bottle of sherry, and a cold chicken.
You say that Wordsworth first awakened you
to the beauty of a sunset. You're mixing
your metaphors, again.
And what am I doing here with you
in this cold inn. You can have your China orange.

William, I want to return to Vermont
and walk three miles to a winter farmhouse.
In January, in Vermont, no one thinks
to criticize a hedgerow or black cattle.
And furthermore within this farmhouse
there's a friend, a Jew, who awakened me
to you; and sure, why not, to winter sunsets also.

The Killigrew Wood

For the Weingartens

We've taken our burlap sacks and entered
the Killigrew Wood.
We're gathering winter mushrooms. We have faith
in what grows wild, what might poison us.
Miss Warminister is here exercising
her hounds. We'll start foraging in the south
and walk clear through to Northparks and the road.
(The hunters pass with headless game

bouncing at their belts. Their valuable animal hides.)
Here, these pliers will pull the burrs
from your coat. (What have you
discovered beneath that log,
among the puffballs. Is it a woman or a young orphan.)
William, you mustn't look up. I'm walking backwards
through wet leaves and brush. We sober at these homicides.

Pitt Poetry Series

James Den Boer, *Learning the Way*
 (1967 U.S. Award of the International Poetry Forum)
James Den Boer, *Trying to Come Apart*
Jon Anderson, *Looking for Jonathan*
Jon Anderson, *Death & Friends*
John Engels, *The Homer Mitchell Place*
Samuel Hazo, *Blood Rights*
David P. Young, *Sweating Out the Winter*
 (1968 U.S. Award of the International Poetry Forum)
Fazıl Hüsnü Dağlarca, *Selected Poems*
 (Turkish Award of the International Poetry Forum)
Jack Anderson, *The Invention of New Jersey*
Gary Gildner, *First Practice*
Gary Gildner, *Digging for Indians*
David Steingass, *Body Compass*
Shirley Kaufman, *The Floor Keeps Turning*
 (1969 U.S. Award of the International Poetry Forum)
Michael S. Harper, *Dear John, Dear Coltrane*
Ed Roberson, *When Thy King Is A Boy*
Gerald W. Barrax, *Another Kind of Rain*
Abbie Huston Evans, *Collected Poems*
Richard Shelton, *The Tattooed Desert*
 (1970 U.S. Award of the International Poetry Forum)
Adonis, *The Blood of Adonis*
 (Syria-Lebanon Award of the International Poetry Forum)
Norman Dubie, *Alehouse Sonnets*

COLOPHON

The poems in this volume are set in Palatino types, a face designed by Her-
mann Zapf and aptly named for the Italian scribe. The cutting used here is the
Linotype version, which is slightly heavier than the handset or film types.
The book is printed from the type on Warren's Olde Style wove paper by
Heritage Printers, Inc., and bound in Columbia Fictionette cloth. The design
is by Gary Gore.